C.S.T BOYD

Mindset is Everything

You Have the POWER to CHANGE YOUR MIND

Contents

1

Dedication

First and Foremost, if anyone would've told me that I would be writing a book and letting the world see and read it, I would've said ," You are out of your mind!" But now look ..I have a book.. So I guess I'm out of my mind but in a great way. I'm learning to take the limits off of myself and giving myself permission to do things I've never done even if I have no clue how it will manifest. What is there to lose? Nothing

I would like to Dedicate this book to everyone that has been connected to me in some way or another. You all have played a part in my life's journey, and even though in that present time I didn't understand a lot of things and the why behind it …. Especially when it comes to the hurt and pain because who loves going through that? I can say now being on that path of getting wisdom and understanding, I am very grateful for each and everyone of you. Not just for all the good but for all of the not so good as well. I pray that your life is full of blessings and that God will grant you the desires of your heart more than you can ever think or imagine.

To my Support Team,

I don't know where I would be without you all in my life. Thank you for the hard conversations, even though I didn't want to hear it at times. Thank you for the love that you all showed in so many forms. Thank you for your uniqueness that only God himself designed for you to have. I love each and every one of you and I thank you so much for believing in me, being, and staying a part of my life. You are with me and in my heart forever.

To the Ones that Brought me into this world. I love and miss you both so much. Even as the tears are forming in my eyes, wishing you both were here right now to see this. I know you are proud. I will forever keep your love,encouraging words, push,striving for the best even in difficult times of conversations in my mind and heart. I love you.

2

Introduction

This journey that is we call LIFE consists of so many many different paths and avenues that require much training and discipline in growth to accomplish in becoming our best authentic selves. Everything that happens in our life doesn't happen by accident. As much as we would like to just have an issue free life, we are not exempt from problems that occur. Life is relational and whether you believe it or not, it's spiritual. We have the gift of CHOICE, and what we decide in that gift at most times can affect our present and majority of the time...our future.We can not stop what is meant to happen in our lives but there are some areas of prevention that we can help ourselves in, if we make the choice to do so.

This journey is not made to be easy but it can be enjoyable, pleasant, thriving, and peaceful even in the difficult times as they come. You ask....How is that ? Where do I start? How do I get there? First I will like to inform you, if you don't already know that With God , All things...not some things.. But ALL things are possible. It starts with that part of you that thinks, that part of you that reasons, the part of you that understands, the part of you that feels, the part of you that

perceives, the part of you that wills ,and the part of you that remembers.
The answer is ……..…**YOUR MIND.**

Let's put on our swim gear and get ready to ride these waves because they are coming. Some little ones and some full force.. You got what it takes... don't give up.
    Let's go.....

"IT IS TIME TO REBUILD, RESTORE, RENEW YOUR MIND AND YOUR WAY OF THINKING."

3

Chapter 1

The Mind

When it comes to the mind, I always tend to think of an iceberg. We know that when we visibly see an iceberg (in reality or picture), that we only see a portion of it and know that it runs so much deeper underneath that water line. We really won't know how large or deep it is unless we go below the surface. Let's dive in....

One Of The Most Powerful Weapons in Your Life

There's so much power in this area of our human body that a lot of us have failed to realize how powerful it really is. Whatever you tell yourself, whether that be in a positive,negative, productive, or destructive, etc manner you have the power to believe it or not believe it. You have the power to shift it to another narrative or stay in it. The choice is always yours but the struggle to change it is also real. This power that you hold together with what you imagine can allow you to create opportunities or obstacles, happiness or unhappiness, peace within yourself or war with yourself, success or failure. The key words in this is "YOU HAVE THE POWER".

It starts with you.

Some of the scientific language that describes the aspects of the mind when we do our research (I'm no scientist) is known as the conscious mind (present mind that you are currently aware of including your thoughts thereof) , the subconscious mind (your storehouse of memories, traumas, good and bad experiences), and the unconscious mind (holds your attitude, beliefs, habits,behaviors) which this in itself have so many level and layers into it but for simplicity sake let's just stick with the basic functions of how we use our mind. We operate so much on our thoughts,feelings and desires and at times refuse to get deeper into and dissect why we think the way we think, why we feel the way we feel, and why we desire the things we desire.

Please ask yourself,
  Why do I think this way?
  Why do I want this in my life?
  What makes me desire this?
  What really makes me feel this way?
  How did I get to this point in my mind?

While you're asking yourself these questions, the very thing that must happen is that you have to be HONEST/TRUTHFUL with yourself in the whys, the what, and even the how. Some things may be simple and then some things may be down right ugly and messy. Have you ever heard the saying " If you want better, you'll do better" , as true as that saying may be to the extent it is, please know that if you "Change your thoughts, you can change your life."

Operating in Mindfulness

Mindfulness is a state of mind in which you are paying close attention to something. Another word to sum that up to is to be attentive. Are you Attentive? Are you present as moments are occurring in your life?

We live a lot in our thoughts and it drives our minds to be either emotional, reasonable or wise. At times we operate in a state of mind where our emotions take over hence being wise and reasoning takes a back seat. We allow anger, sadness, frustration, irritation, fear ,etc to govern our decision making in our everyday lives.

When we live a life like this ,it affects everyone around us including our own lives even down to our health. Aren't you tired of that? Do you want to change your mindset? Are you tired of getting on your own nerves?

STORY TIME

I had a friend that was in a very toxic relationship and everytime we would get together we would discuss what had happened and come up with a resolve to try to make it better. The whole time I knew if I tried to change the conversation it would gradually get back to conversing about the relationship. It was very draining for me at times but I had to get into the mind frame that my friend is hurting and they just want to be heard, seen and loved, especially by their significant other but then at the same time digging a little bit deeper knowing that my friend had some things going on within as well causing them to stay in this relationship. I paid very close attention to things that were said to realize that it was bigger and deeper than the relationship at hand. It stemmed from abandonment, rejection, abuse during childhood, not feeling like they were enough, verbal and physical abuse as an adult ,etc. Their significant other made them feel all of those things by their words and or actions. For the life of me I didn't understand why my friend would stay in such toxicity. After expressing how I felt and the effect it was having on me, my friend expressed that this was seen growing up and it was all they knew. Nobody ever explained that it wasn't a healthy relationship nor did my friend have the tools to get out or know how to handle this situation. I had to become very mindful in order to be wise in what I said or did next because my friend's heart was very fragile. We had to have the hard conversations in order for my friend to become mindful about their emotions and how it was affecting our friendship because this toxic relationship was taking over our friendship. We didn't laugh or have fun anymore. Even though my friend was physically there in my face, being present in the moment(s) every time we went to hang out was non-existent. Being mindful in this situation had to run both ways in order for us to get to a better place.

In this situation, we knew it was toxic but I also called it dysfunction. We all have some form of dysfunction connected to us whether be in our own families, friends or even within ourselves. Nobody is perfect.This concern starts to rise up when

dysfunction starts to become normalized. This is when things start to transpire more frequently than it should and it's not beneficial to your life that results in pain,strife,no peace, dis-ease, negativity, etc, to which it starts to become a level of comfort even though it causes your heart emotional pain, causing health issues, being in a mental prison, can't function at your best and causing you not to feel free so much so that you start to accept it as normal. Like life is supposed to be this way.

Let me be the first to say if you haven't heard it already.. It's NOT!!

Even though we are promised troubles in our lives doesn't mean we have to stay stuck in suffering part of that trouble. How are you handling troubles as it comes your way? Are you playing victim? Are you having a pity party for yourself and want everyone else to feel sorry for you?

"Awareness is very important"

4

Chapter 2

Hurt, Trauma,Pain

It's okay to feel the emotions and embrace them behind what doesn't feel good or what may not go your way but don't stay there too long and allow yourself to become the emotion and allow it to govern your life. Let's just say that If you allow that to happen, what you are doing is setting yourself up for a spiraling hole of destruction and self sabotage while it piles more negative emotions on top of negative emotions until one day you realize.. I'm not OK and you have to fight to get yourself out of that hole. Meanwhile, life is still happening and troubles are still coming your way.

Let's do an illustration…time to imagine…

Imagine yourself in a wide 10 ft deep hole with dirt all around you and as life happens, good and difficult, where wood blocks represent good or difficult and rain represents the challenges or blessings of your life. I'm going to let you choose how you decide to see it. You are trying to figure 1st why you are in this hole and how you can get out. What usually happens first when we are not in a situation that we feel like isn't satisfying for our circumstance. Maybe anger and frustration presents itself, then the tears start flowing because sadness kicks in due to the fact we can't see how we got into this hole and there is no one there to physically help us out. So now you feel stuck then it's a back and forth battle with anger and sadness. In your own strength you then try to climb your way out bypassing several wood blocks and the dirt is a little moist in some areas more than others so about ½ way up you slip causing you to slide back down to the bottom. You try this multiple times and you get tired. You yell, you scream but no one can hear you. Hours go by and you try again and in that attempt you fail. At this point you're really angry and you're sitting in that anger for hours using up your energy to continue to try to get out. You find yourself blaming people for getting you in this situation and start thinking about how they treated you which resulted in how you treated them. Then decide to calm and quiet yourself mentally. Your mind at this point is not making sense of anything. Something pops up in your mind that brings you into a thought about what you can do and what you have done and you decide to focus on you. You at some point say a prayer and ask God to help you get out. Some more time passes and as you sit in your quietness you finally see the wood blocks that have been there all along.

Do you see so far in this illustration how being so caught up in anger and sadness and whatever other negative emotional feeling that we decide to stay stuck in can make our situation more difficult to see how we can succeed in getting out of a particular circumstance? Do you see how you can be blinded by the very thing that can help you? How are you using your mind to operate in difficult times? Back to the illustration exercise..

You notice the blocks and you get happy because now you can get out. You start stacking the blocks in the wall of the hole and as you're forcing the blocks in, some are staying and some are slipping which makes you grow back into frustration, irritation and anger. You go through the same cycle that you did at the beginning when you first entered the hole several times and at this point you are tired of getting angry and sad. So now you get to the place of thought and question yourself "Why am I here and how did I get here?" You shifted your thoughts to you now. What have I done to put myself in this situation? As you ponder on that you realize the errors you've made in your life, your thoughts started diving into how your childhood and how it shaped your adulthood, you've been abused,neglected, unloved, rejected, betrayed,etc and you never healed from those things as well as not realizing it was even an issue. So you sit in that and cry out but this time not from anger but from pain. You start to feel convicted about how you treated everyone in your life. Also while in that feeling You hear a gentle voice that says " Forgiveness". So it hits you that you must forgive those that have hurt you. It starts to rain and it pours. The dirt is turning into mud and all the blocks that were staying put are now slipping out of the holes. You think to yourself "I'm never getting out of here" and "why should i forgive the people that hurt me and they're not even sorry for what they did?" You sit in that for a while and look up as you see the sun coming out and you hear "Freedom". You have no clue what that means right now because you are back and forth again with your anger, sadness and now added on to that is the hurt, pain,and trauma you've experienced.

You start to question and get mad at God for allowing this to happen to you but not realizing this situation needed to happen in order for you to see YOU.

We have all encountered some form of hurt, pain and or trauma. Whether those things came from family, friends, strangers, pastors, churches, the workplace,etc it is our responsibility to heal. It's our responsibility to know our triggers and work on those things until it gets to a place where you're not triggered or hurt anymore. A lot of us are filtering things in our lives right now that happened to us 10+ years ago that we are still holding on to and haven't forgiven people for. The act of forgiveness is hard but it can be done and your freedom relies on it. When we hold on to unforgiveness it causes our minds to have a different perspective and at times a warped perception of others in our lives even if they never caused us any harm. Aren't you tired of hurting? Aren't you tired of feeling like you're in a mental prison with your own emotions?

I'm here to let you know that you can get out of it.

There is a way out.

It's not going to be easy and you are going to have to work at it

It is worth it at the end of it all.

Don't you want to be free mentally, emotionally and spiritually?

Back to Illustration…

You come to a calm state of mind.. After talking to yourself for a length of time and believing that you are going to get out of this hole, you are determined to do what you need to do to break through and reach the top. You start placing the blocks back in the wall of the hole, some areas have dried some are still wet. You shift your mind into a "let me see this as an opportunity to be patient with this situation instead of an obstacle including all these wet spots that these blocks can't fit into as of yet." Your mind continues to shift as you are working these blocks in the wall of the hole to stay put and as you are doing so you are say to yourself I forgive this person, i forgive that person, I forgive, i forgive, i forgive, and even down to you asking God to forgive you all the wrong you have done.

You start to notice little holes in the wall and they look like the size of the blocks. You take a block and place it in the hole and to your surprise it stays in place cause you have more steps to get you higher to the top of this hole to get out and be free. Once you are out, you come to the realization that this situation had to happen in order to gain a shift in your mind and also your perspective has shifted and your attitude is different.

Now in life it's not always that simple to get out of the normalized dysfunction or to heal from those who have hurt you. As in the illustration you can see that a repetitive cycle transpired and kept you stuck and anytime that happens it is like you have to start over and you do. It's not until you get to a place in your mind where you are tired of being sick and tired even getting on your own nerves and how you act and respond to things because the result of your response is hardly beneficial to a situation especially in conflict. Once you are tired enough, you will shift mentally and change.

It's Time To Heal

A good friend of mine shared something with me and I would like to share it with you. When it comes to forgiveness and how to heal.

The meaning of forgiveness is an act of your will and it releases the feelings of resentment and even revenge toward someone/situation that has hurt you. It releases the power and the control that the person(s) and situations have transpired in your life even if they're not deserving.

Holding on to unforgiveness is a sentence to being in prison in your mind and there is no freedom. On the spiritual side of things it gives the enemy stamina to create a foothold in your life to keep you stuck in bitterness, anger, resentment and that will hinder you from growing, healing and getting the best life that you deserve to live and becoming your best self that you can possibly be.

1."Don't nurse it"-don't constantly think on memories of pain it brought

2."Don't curse it"- don't speak against it because it may benefit your growth

3."Disperse it"- separate yourself from it

4."Give it to God and he will reverse it"- as if it never happened

Even if you have to continue to repeat this to yourself in order to believe it and train yourself until you start to apply it to your life and your situations. You will start noticing that you're making progress.

Sometimes we have to train ourselves to get out of an old way of thinking in order to operate in a new way of movement.

"The mind governed by the flesh is death, but the mind governed by the Spirit is life and peace."

5

Chapter 3

Make a Decision

Again i say, It all starts will you!

You have to make a decision to Heal!

You have to make a decision that you will not be bitter!

You will have to make a decision that you will not operate out of anger!

You have to make a decision that you will be your best self!

You will have to make a decision to forgive those who hurt you!

You will have to make a decision to make the effort!

You will have to make the decision to get out of your funk!

You will have to make the decision that you will no longer be manipulated!

You will have to make the decision that you will live your best life!

You will have to make the decision to get closer to God!

You will have to make the decision to know who and whose you are!

You will have to make the decision that you will no longer allow the enemy to use your mind!

You will have to make the decision that you will live in peace!

You will have to make the decision that you will be happy!

You will have to make the decision that you will no longer allow circumstances to shake your world!
   You will have to make the decision that you will no longer think negatively!

You will have to make the decision that you will renew your mind everyday!

You have to make the decision to stick to and commit to your decisions!
   You will have to make the decision that you will govern your thoughts and not allow the enemy to speak lies to you!

You will have to make the decision to operate in your God given authority!

You will have to make the decision to seek God's face everyday!

You will have to make the decision not fall for the enemies traps and schemes!

You will have to make a decision to operate in mindfulness!

You have to make the decision to be present in the moment!

You have to make the decision to die to yourself daily!

You have to make the decision to give yourself grace in the process!

You have to make the decision to be patient in your process!

You have to make a decision to forgive yourself for the errors you've made!

You have to make a decision not to allow situations to stress you!

You have to make a decision that your no means yes and your yes means yes!

You have to make the decision that you will not settle!

You have to make the decision that you will not give up!

You have to make the decision to be humble!

You have to make the decision to not operate in pride and ego!

You have to make the decision to be teachable!

You have to make the decision to get counseling and apply for it!

You have to make the decision that it's OK not to be OK!

You have to make the decision to put God first!
   You have to make a decision to take your POWER back!

Whatever your decisions are please know that You have to make the decision that intel the decisions you make are beneficial for your life so that you may live it more abundantly than you can ever think or imagine for God is the one who is able to do far more for you than you can do for yourself.

In making all of these decisions plus the ones that may reveal itself as you continue to live and experience life there's one major of a few other major things that must happen constantly everyday in order to achieve that life you want and that is DYING TO SELF.

This means in your new way of thinking, new mindset,all around newness in your thought process you will have things that come up in everyday life that will try to get you back into your old way of doing things. It is a lifelong process because we grow and learn everyday. Simplifying even more, Dying to Self is denying yourself of things that you may want to do and or desire to have that may not be beneficial to you short term and or long term.
   Some Examples of that may be..
   You decided to go on a fast, you are hungry and want to eat but you made a decision to fast and your body is craving food. You must die to yourself to get to your end goal.
   Same with dieting, You made a decision that you will not eat

bread,pasta,cookies or cake and you are craving it badly.. You must die to yourself to accomplish what you set out to accomplish..

Someone at your job is being rude and has been rude and you just want to give them a piece of your mind or put the paws on him or her but even though it may feel good in the moment the end result may be you losing your job and then you will be mad at yourself for allowing them to trigger you to that point.

Let's say you're married and your spouse did or said something and you are triggered and because that's your spouse, there's nothing wrong with expressing yourself right? This one is a little bit more about being mindful and not to say the others are not but this one is about timing, the tone in which you say,and considering the fact of what your spouse may or may not be experiencing that caused them to say or do something that triggered you and also what you may be experiencing that cause you to be triggered.

This (4) can run a little deeper but all and all it's about being mindful in all the areas listed.

It's not easy but whatever it is that you need to do not to revert back to old ways then do it. If you have to take a moment and scream then scream, if you have to take a moment and pray then pray, pause , evaluate before speaking,etc. it does get easier as time goes on but it's still not easy if that makes sense.

"No Weapon Formed Against You Shall Prosper"

6

Chapter 4

Be Intentional

It is very important and crucial to your life that we learn how to govern (take authority of) our mind and emotions. Have you ever heard of the saying "Battleground of Your Mind". This is an everyday work in itself because you have experienced so much and have yet to experience more. You remember in the Introduction of this book, I stated that life is relational but it's also spiritual? This is when that spirit part really sets in and takes place. We can not do this life in our own strength because honestly we are just not that capable to fight by ourselves day in and day out for the rest of our lives. I'm sure you have tried and i can bet you got exhausted and keep getting exhausted.

Contrary to what others may think, there is a spirit world out there and we have no clue all that it entails, but what I do know is that there is a battle going on and it's not against flesh and blood but against spiritual forces of evil in the heavenly places so we must put on the whole armor of God so that we may be able to stand against the schemes of the enemy.

The enemy survives in mental chaos and causes mental torment and his goal is to conquer your mind. If there's disorder then there is confusion then those emotions are haywire that mind becomes a playground for the enemy to have a good time in.

Everyday we get up we must make the decision about how we go about our day on purpose. We must be deliberate about how we treat people, handle conflict, how we think especially when things do go our way. We must be intentional about how we go about life.We have to build up our spirit mind (another level of the mind). Do you read the word of God everyday (this feeds your spirit)? This life is beyond just you. The enemy has a way to torment your mind even the things we may deem to be small. Do you find yourself trying to make sense of everything and if it doesn't then it must be wrong? Are you a " I depend on me and I know my own plans" type of person? Here's another good one, are you an overthinker, where you make everything so small so big?

What this does is block and build walls to your spirit mind. These are some types of battlegrounds we all struggle with and don't realize. God wants you to be free. When we operate like these few things I just mentioned we have placed ourselves in agreement with these battlegrounds and we must come out of it.

Constantly getting in your feelings causes the mind to be tossed back and forth, back and forth, and back and forth some more.We must heal from these battlegrounds.

When a thought enters into your mind that makes you go on an emotional rant (anger, pain, frustration, stress,etc) we must captivate the thought and not feed it and ask God to expose you to you and what you need to do in order to change. It's time to know who you really are so you can activate that power and authority that's within you. Discovering your true self as you draw closer to God will make you feel like you can accomplish anything, but you must do the work and know that God is with you every step of the way. It may seem like nothing is happening but know that it is. Think of when you're planting a flower. As you water it and tend to it the roots are growing even though you can't see it but it's happening and after sometime you will start seeing a bud of the flower surface to the top. It's the same with your growth and healing. Always remember faith without works is dead and that with God, all things are possible. You have to trust and believe. Make a conscious decision about your healing. Be intentional about your growth.Inner work is challenging. Getting to the core of you is a daily, consistent, persistent effort that we must be aware of and operate in.

Changing Your Perspective Can Change Your Life

Your mental view in a situation/circumstance when you choose to see the good in the bad, to give grace when you want to yell, scream, or possibly get violent, seeing an opportunity to handle a situation in wisdom instead of treating it like an obstacle. There will be days where you fall but you get back up and evaluate and become aware of what is, what was, and how you can go about it differently next time. Learn how to give yourself grace in the process because healing doesn't happen overnight. If you are the type of person where you get triggered in frustration easily and it's nothing for you to "pop off" on a person that crosses you, it may take some time to calm that down. What may take you 2 secs may now take you 15 secs to get to the "pop off" trigger. Progress is progress and if you keep working at it and training your mind to think and do better, you will realize one day that you're not popping off on anybody anymore. You will be so proud of yourself as you continue to evaluate you and become aware of your triggers.

Awareness is so important in growth and healing as well. Not just awareness in others but awareness of yourself (mind,body,soul). The giant you must defeat when it comes to your mind is YOU! You must confront yourself in the mirror. As humans, once we create a visual in our mind, we tend to start to believe the thoughts entering in then we start speaking on it, next we start acting on it then ultimately it changes in to that thing (positive or negative, good or bad) Once you know who you are, what others think of you won't even matter if it does to you now. What others do think of you is none of your business anyway. At the end of day, What you think of you is what really matters. It's time to get free and operate in your God given authority that you carry on the inside.

If you are afraid then do it afraid. If you are nervous then do it in your nervousness. You have nothing to lose but everything to gain for you and within you.

"Control how you respond to things sent to destroy your peace."

7

Chapter 5

Set Your Mind ABLAZE

L et's go about this in a slightly different approach from all the nuggets in the previous chapters. Ask yourself, What's the one thing that gets you going? I mean really gets you going? What motivates you to the point you look forward to getting out of bed each morning and getting at it! That thing you would do and not even stress over profiting from it (monetarily) if it came down to it? If you can't answer that question right off it's ok you have the time to think about it from this point on. A lot of people think they have to have some grande or magnificent idea in order to get something moving and shaking and often times partially paralyze themselves mentally because although they want to think big and do big things; (and there is absolutely nothing wrong with wanting that) there are times when you have to start with the spark and work that spark until it becomes a full flame. Your mind is your greatest asset! Whatever direction you set it in is the direction everything is going to go. EVERYTHING starts in the mind. It's like a car or boat or motorcycle or even a plane!, whatever direction you have them go is the direction they are going because you are controlling them.

The Mission in this operation is your MENTAL FREEDOM.

How bad do you really want it and what would you do to get it? A lot of the things we struggle with come from old mess. Are you willing to get down and dirty with your own mess in order to get to this FREEDOM because that's what it's going to take. Nobody can make you want it, you are going to have to want it bad enough for yourself. Yes you will have to feel the emotions that come with confronting certain issues that have occurred in your life but know that where the pain is, the healing dwells there too. Embrace those emotions and keep in the forefront of your mind that you have a mission to accomplish and you will get there by any means necessary for the Freedom of your Mind. Nobody wants to stay (if they are honest with themselves) in a state of mind that results in agony and misery.

My encouragement to you is that YOU GOT THIS! You don't have to do this alone and it's not made for you to do all alone. Yes the work you must do is much but there are so many people in this world who are going through what you may be going through. Some may have gone through it, healed, and prospered further mentally and are helping others to get to that place as well. You can do anything you put your mind to. Do your research, seek counsel, do the work and ***DON'T GIVE UP***! You just may be getting positioned to help someone get through in the future.

"Activate That Warrior Inside of You Now!
It's time to Conquer The Battlegrounds Of Your Mind"

8

Conclusion and Thank You

I would like to take this time out to say thank you to those of you that took your time to read my book. The Journey of Life is a path of ups and downs and rounds and rounds that I walk every single day as well as you. I don't have it all together and I battle within myself like the next person. Writing and reading this book is also a reminder for me. Sometimes we all need that reminder in order to get that push to go further than where we are at the current moment. The more you know who you are and what you want , the less you let things upset you. Stay patient and trust your journey while giving yourself much grace. Remember it's a Process.

*"Healing begins at the moment you stop pretending you aren't hurt."

*"The wounds are probably not your fault but the healing is your responsibility."

*Confrontation of self leads to discovery and inner truth. If we're afraid to confront ourselves, we can't move forward in a positive and productive manner."

* *"No longer responding or reacting to people who trigger you is one of the ways you strengthen your spiritual muscles."*

* *"You are free to choose but you are not free from the consequences of your choice."*

* *"Train your mind to be calm in every situation."*

Quick prayers:

I release everything that I've allowed to come into my mind and take away my peace. I give myself permission to be the joyful, fearless, powerful man/woman I was created to be. I'm getting free from mental chaos TODAY!

I have a sound mind and I will not be tormented by my mistakes, disappointment, or fears any longer. I forgive myself for allowing my mind to be taken over and caught up in the tornado of frustration, anger, confusion, worry, doubt, etc. Everyday I will show up and do my best within the roles I play in my life. Everything will be ok and I'm so blessed.

In Jesus' Name
  Amen

9

Resources

Bible gateway. (1993). Bible. Retrieved August 7, 2022, from https://www.biblegateway.com/

diffen. (2022, August 4). Subconscious vs. Unconscious mind. Https://Www.Diffen.Com/Difference/Subconscious_vs_Unconscious_mind. Retrieved August 7, 2022, from https://www.diffen.com/difference/Subconscious_vs_Unconscious_mind

Marra, G. M. (2021, November 11). 9 interesting facts about your subconscious mind. Retrieved August 7, 2022, from https://www.gailmarrahypnotherapy.com/9-interesting-facts-about-your-subconscious-mind/#:~:text=The%20Subconscious%20Mind%20controls%2095%20percent%20of%20your%20life&text=Todays%20science%20estimates%20that%2095,that%20lies%20beyond%20conscious%20awareness

Merriam webster. (n.d.). Merriam Webster Dictionary. Retrieved August 7, 2022, from https://www.merriam-webster.com/

Unconscious. (n.d.). Unconscious. Retrieved August 7, 2022, from https://www.psychologytoday.com/us/basics/unconscious#how-the-unconscious-mind-works